While Mercury Fish

poems by

Ana C. H. Silva

Finishing Line Press
Georgetown, Kentucky

While Mercury Fish

Copyright © 2020 by Ana C. H. Silva
ISBN 978-1-64662-259-7 First Edition
All rights reserved under International and Pan-American Copyright Conventions. No part of this book may be reproduced in any manner whatsoever without written permission from the publisher, except in the case of brief quotations embodied in critical articles and reviews.

ACKNOWLEDGMENTS

"Street Feather" previously appeared in August, 2015 in *Chronogram*.
"The Best Way I Can Explain It" previously appeared in *Abyss & Apex* Issue 71 (July 2019).
An early version of "A Poem About Storks" previously appeared in *Small Batch*, a The Poetry Distillery echapbook.

With gratitude to Stacey Balkun, Jenn Givhan, Beth Bigler, and Josh Dorman.

Publisher: Leah Maines
Editor: Christen Kincaid
Cover Art: Ana C. H. Silva
Author Photo: Ana C. H. Silva
Cover Design: Elizabeth Maines McCleavy

Order online: www.finishinglinepress.com
also available on amazon.com

Author inquiries and mail orders:
Finishing Line Press
P. O. Box 1626
Georgetown, Kentucky 40324
U. S. A.

Table of Contents

The Best Way I Can Explain It 1

This Train 2

1980s 3

1990s 4

2000s 5

2020s 6

Underneath This Note Is a Blanket 7

A Poem About Storks 8

100 Year Old Eggs 9

9/11/01 10

Aluminum 11

Nasty 12

Street Feather 13

Red Button 14

to all those who resist hate with love

The Best Way I Can Explain It

is that there are no more magic shows. I watched them as a kid, sometimes all night, into the morning. The scratchy carpet, the rabbit-eared TV. The birds appearing in fists, just closed around a coin. I'd watch them without wanting to, clicking past 70s sexcapades, tall-hatted sepia cowboys with their billowing freight trains. I saw the ladies sawn in half, their sparkling dresses whole again. The green umbrella appears where nothing was. The endless, endless satin handkerchiefs, tied into a rainbow and another and another sailing through the air. The top hat and the black and white wand. But the woman will one day be unable to carry on the act, will tear off the sequins that scratch her skin, enlist the help of a stained-card, cut-rate divorce lawyer, set up shop as a hairdresser in the next town. *When the fire's moving, it can sound like a freight train.* She raises her kids on her own, lets them see their deadbeat dad only when she wants to go out at night. She'll wonder what the hell she was doing all those years in that man's pasteboard boxes that smelled like dust and glue. The sound of a moving fire is like a freight train. A tsunami can sound like a freight train. One day it will hit her. She will cry out and scream. Her own rage rattling her chest will startle her. The cries that come out of her belly and bring her to her knees for a moment will scare and energize her. *Many witnesses have said a tsunami sounds like a freight train.* She will find her voice, beyond all reason, beyond all thought, the loudest thing ever heard, breaking glass TVs in everyone's living room as she hustles her children into the night, into the next town and the next and the next, searching for something more than this.

This train

   is not making the stop
      she will blow her horn into the future
         startle people standing
            on the edge
               and not stop
                  and really
                       not stop

1980s

I stockpiled my favorite
Almay medium concealer
concerned most of all that I
could cover my zits in a crisis.

At least my face would not offend
the others while we ran out of fossil fuels.

1990s

I would have grabbed
my favorite black Calvin Klein
jeans and second-hand European
philosophy books.

At least I'd say intelligent things, while looking hot
while we ran out of clean water.

2010s

It's my children
I'd want to grab
and what on earth
do we do with that.

While mercury fish float, stunned, in a tsunami.
While shattering earthquakes level cities
on my old quaint bucket list.

2020s

The East River finally did it, came bubbling to our building, *Renaissance East*, flooded all the electricals. No hot showers, no heat. Muddy water up to my legs and my daughters' waists when we investigate the dark street. There are no saviors, I always knew that, but we had working light switches, soft, dry beds, internet, Netflix. Fat Fresh Direct orders arrived in excessive numbers of card board boxes I wish I had now to line my floors which I can no longer clean. My larger palm and fingers fold and press, sticky and warm, their smaller palms and fingers, in the cold air, trying not to lose them in the scene: the people yelling and crying, looking ragged, looking done with everything, and yet it could be so much worse than this, it always could, really it could.

Trying not to squeeze
their little fingers
too hard.

Underneath This Note Is a Blanket

I remember the little children with dirty tote bags begging for over-ripe fruit. They always asked for that, or stale bread. I didn't know if our cans would last, if our space heater would stop glowing. I could not risk disease. We had an extra room, though, and I knew my old self would have held one tight to my chest, sour smell and greasy hair, the fear of lice and fleas no matter at all. My old self, if she did exist, would have been unable to let the child go, to hear her make quiet knocks on other unreceptive doors.

Were you one of those children? I know you have been to starvation and back; I can see it in your eyes. Did you have a red wool cardigan with a sprinkle of moth holes at the bottom? It seemed so old-fashioned, from a time when people sat around warm hearths, decorated with personal knicknacks, blazing lights on in all the rooms, a roast in their ovens while they knitted loved ones sweaters they didn't really need.

We live in a time where it's hard to be a good person. That's not an excuse. I'm sorry for what I did. I ignored the knocks, or briskly handed out small bags of old food with a quickly shut door.

What we shared last night—the bowl of hot ramen, the almost-tasty apple, your half bag of M&Ms, our conversation about poetry—when was the last time I'd talked of that?—and especially your warmth in the night, the good night hug, the nearness you gave me on the shared bed—was the first time I've relaxed since my children left.

The blanket is from me. It's a good one.

A Poem about Storks

You will never know.
You will never understand the thing.

You were there.
They may have come out of your body

or someone else's.
You fed them with your dripping breasts

or dripping bottle nipple.

Maybe you even know the exact
moment they came

but they didn't come, then, not exactly.
There's no way to pin it down.

Your children may be with you now
or they may be gone

—Either way they are not
within your grasp—

You will never understand.
I promise you.

100 Year Old Eggs

I remember with some fondness
the Chinatown shop with the hanging fish,
the black translucence of 100 year old eggs
nestled in a tall wooden barrel.

The dark green sheen outside
the squishy lighter green insides.

As a child I wondered was this
my flesh in 100 years?

9/11/01

Looking back, that felt like the beginning of something.

They evacuated the Empire State Building just in case.

We hugged under the thick quilt of our bed
    quiet, like brothers.

The sound of rain hitting the air conditioner:
    like a building, after its destruction

descending upon us
in sharp hard
flakes.

Aluminum

It's hard not to think some of this liquid is backwash
from inside their mouths. Those people who voted them in.

Their spit runs all over our hands, wets
our forearms   pant legs   sandaled feet.

We keep shaking out, stashing the sun-bleached cans
in thin, ragged plastic bags

It's hard not to think some of this liquid is backwash
from inside their mouths. Those people who voted them in.

Their spit runs all over our hands, wets
our forearms   pant legs   sandaled feet.

We keep shaking out, stashing the sun-bleached cans
in thin, ragged plastic bags.

The water seeps back into
the small holes
of the land

Nasty

She can just see a large animal
          in the grip of her nostrils. All night
she gasps and chokes her outrage.

He is nowhere
everywhere
          breaking leaves tantalizing

snapping twigs
     messing up the dirt
               of her yard.   She seizes his brazenness
               over and over with wide open nose

cloudy air gusts

venting evenly

between her

salivating

pearl white

teeth.

Street Feather

                        It's
                        easy
       to spot bright
                blue and red, or
           spotted
                against the dark grain
     of the concrete.
          Scrape your finger against
 the pavement
         when you pick it up.
Bring it close to your eyes,
       see sticky fibers
     locking tiny
              strands of feather into
    feather.
             Each mini feather is a
    feather itself.
               Brown tips signal disease
     or contagion.
                   You might not want to touch it,
   and many people don't,
                but don't forget
     this is exactly the part
              of the whole long feather
that connects to—
               —that made it—
           t
           h
           e
           b
           i
           r
           d.

Red Button

The sign under the red button said
to talk   press   and release
wait for sound response

Everyone else in the car
had a blank look in their eye
I pressed it because I wanted
to feel the air again.
I almost remembered the feeling of air
but it had been an age an eon
at least a dozen years.

We waited for the sound response
as we had so many times before.
Ten times, a hundred times
maybe only once.
Generally we heard our own breathing
in our hearts and other people's shuffling shoes
kicking old newspapers under the seats.

It crackled this time.
People crowded to see the red button glow.
The sound of the crackle
echoed off the rounded metal walls
shot off the greyed-in windows
came back into our ears.

Someone is behind that rusted
tin cup they are talking into
the one attached to
the string connected to
the cup I am
hearing out of right now.
It had been a year since we'd heard the sound of another voice
an endless fortnight, maybe forever.

We knew the smell of each other's breath by heart.
Even in the low light we knew who was standing closest to us.
Someone is there in the cup asking
Are you are okay
everyone nods, smiling in front of their sweat.
I say yes, we are okay.
We have been down here a century, a decade, a moment.
No one knows why we came here
or what happens after this.

Help is on the way, they shout, rattling the tin can.
You are in need of assistance.
You are at risk.
Just stay where you are and we
will come to you.

We don't know if this is a dream
the rescue fantasy we have re-rehearsed a thousand times
a million times, collectively a billion times
or if we will now be free.

Your weight will feel like nothing to us
we will carry each of you up steep stairs
your waists at our necks
we will hold your legs to our chests
so you don't fall.

My friends, my compatriots, we hug each other all around.
Our body odor has morphed into a collective stench.
It's true that you stop noticing it after a while.
I remembered the sharpness of it at first.
Now it just smelled like people, like animals, like life.

*Thick, hard clothes protect our skin
so we can lift you up
from grime, grease, despair
the hollow echo in your ear.*

*You will breathe the sweet air
You will breathe the sweet air*

Ana C. H. Silva lives in East Harlem, NYC and West Shokan, NY. Her poems are in *Podium, Rogue Agent, The Mom Egg Review, the nth position, Snow Monkey, Chronogram, StepAway Magazine, Anemone Sidecar, Between the Lines, Tinderbox Poetry Journal, The Poetry Distillery, Shantih Journal, Abyss & Apex,* and *Fairytales and Folklore Reimagined*. Ana created *Olive Couplets*, an Olive, NY community-based poetry work, and *Lines in the Woods*, an outdoor, interactive poetry installation at the CHHS in Rosendale, NY. Since 2016, Ana has curated the MER online Gallery. She won the inaugural Rachel Wetzsteon Memorial Poetry Prize at the 92nd St. Y Unterberg Poetry Center. Her 2019 poetry chapbook, *One Cupped Hand Above the Other*, is with Dancing Girl Press.

www.ingramcontent.com/pod-product-compliance
Lightning Source LLC
LaVergne TN
LVHW041526070426
835507LV00013B/1851